THE ULTIMATE
GUIDE TO UNDERSTANDING & GETTING STARTED WITH
SOCIAL MEDIA

SUZZETTE R. TURNBULL

THE ULTIMATE GUIDE

to

UNDERSTANDING

and

GETTING STARTED

WITH SOCIAL MEDIA

SUZZETTE R. TURNBULL

Design by Horace Hord

Cover by Precision Graphic Designs

ISBN-13: 978-1545111444

ISBN-10:1545111448

Printed in the United States of America

First printing this edition 2017

Table of Contents

Acknowledgements

With special thanks:

To God for being my source.

To my sister, Keisha Turnbull, for her love, sacrifices and endless support.

To my mother, Winsome Turnbull, for her unconditional love.

To my father, Douglas Turnbull, for the exemplary example he set for me.

To my brother, Dean Turnbull, for his continued support and encouragement.

To my nephews, Andre, Elijah, and Dean, Jr., for being my pride and joy.

To my best friend, Millie Phaeton, for teaching me what true friendship and sisterhood means.

To Philbert Lake, my big little brother, for his priceless friendship and being a man of valor.

To JAVEN for believing in me.

To Doris Kara Brown, for her dedication to quality results and support of the Uncommon Marketing mission and vision.

To my spiritual father and mentor, Bishop Henry Fernandez, who inspires and pushes me beyond my limits.

To Baron Hilliard for being an example of the power of social media.

To Sharon Beason, CEO of Womeneuer, for the inspiration to write this book and the opportunity to be a part of the WomeneurCollective.

To my Faith Center family for their prayers and support.

To my students for the opportunity to sow into their dreams.

To my Angels for rebuilding me!

FOREWORD

Suzzette Turnbull is a person of extreme integrity and tremendous character with the amazing ability to fight for perfection.

Working with her over the years, I have experienced her gift in action for my companies JCM and Worship in The NOW, Inc.; and I have seen nothing less than excellence and quality.

Suzzette is one of the few people that I admire from beginning to end because of her ability to make something out of nothing with complete and utter integrity.

The advice that she has given, and the direction that she has shown to not only me but to many others, has been priceless. So much so, that anything that she joins is an absolute guaranteed success from the moment she puts her hands on it.

Suzzette is an effective communicator, marketer, and strategist. She is certainly a leading woman of this now generation. I believe that what she shares, and the information that she will bring forth to the public will be so rich and powerful that it will change many generations to come. She is knowledgeable because she has her eye on the prize and her finger on the pulse. It is an exciting time for people like Suzzette, and I am certainly honored to have her as an associate, a colleague, and the ability to call her my friend.

Jáven

Singer/Actor/Speaker

CHAPTER 1

INTRODUCTION TO SOCIAL MEDIA

We live in a world where social media is taking over our lives. According to Pew Research Center, 69 percent of people are using some form of social media. It has become a common activity in our daily routine and a go to source of information for recommendations, political news, breaking news, resources, and information in general. Have you ever seen one of your Facebook friends pose a question looking for help from the Facebook universe?

Well, this usage means the fate of your customers' buying behavior can easily lie in the palm of your hands. Social media has become the first level credit and credibility check for companies. Ask yourself, "Can consumers find me/my business online? If so, is my online presence set up to make the right impression and influence potential consumers to choose me/my business?"

As a business owner, what possibly could you do but to keep up with the times? Before we dig deep, it is important for you to know how many people are actually using social media. There is an average of 1.23 billion daily active users on Facebook (Source: Facebook as of April 2017) and 1.86 billion monthly active users (Source: Zephoria.com).

If Facebook were a country, it would be the most populated country in the world even surpassing China. As much as you may not like it, your mom, your grandmother, your auntie … they are all up on the latest happenings and are now active Facebook users.

Instagram has more than 600 million users with more than 400 million daily active users. (Source: expandedramblings.com). Twitter has 319 million users (Source: expandedramblings.com). Now, these are only three of the top social media platforms. You can only imagine what the user numbers are for Pinterest, Snapchat, and Periscope.

What is social media?

Social media is the process of creating and distributing content on the Internet or networking with other users. Users may access social media platforms via websites, mobile devices, and tablet applications.

What are social media platforms?

Examples of social media platforms are Facebook, LinkedIn, and Twitter, which will be discussed in greater detail along with several others. These platforms are designed to make connecting with people and businesses around the world much easier.

It is easy for you to create a unique identity and engage in a two-way dialogue with whomever you choose. As fantastic as these platforms are, they require you to invest the time to set them up and be active. They are not magical, but they do provide bells and whistles and easy to use features important for accelerating the building of new relationships. The most successful businesses are the ones with the strongest relationships.

Remember two things:

1. **Social media is about relationships.** The same way you engage with people offline is the same way you should engage with them online. Courtesy, respect, and compassion go a long way. More eyes are watching your interactions than you think and see in your numbers.

2. **Keep the "social" in social media.** There are human beings on the other side of your dialogue who look forward to value added interactions.

What are some ways you can use social media?

- **Advertise and increase awareness** of your brand, product, or service to a target audience.

- **Interact, connect, and exchange information** with like-minded individuals.

- **Stay up-to-date** on current events and breaking news.

- **Make it a resource hub.** Follow and engage with accounts that share information.

- **Event promotion** and connecting event attendees by using unique hashtags.

- **Remain in touch** with your customers by being where they are.

Make technology work for you! Follow the brands and the people in whom you are interested. When used correctly, it can become a streamlined way to keep up with the types of news and updates most important to you. It is now easier to keep up with what your competitors are doing as well as identify like-minded people and businesses for potential alliances and partnerships. You have control over your experience.

What are examples of some social media platforms?

There are plethoras of social media platforms, which can be a little overwhelming. Where should I be and how should I use them are frequent dilemmas. It depends on your activity and desired outcome. Below, the most popular sites are categorized to help provide a context and use.

1. **Social networking sites** – Facebook, Google+, Linked-In

2. **Micro-blogging** *(practice of making short, frequent posts)* – Twitter, Tumblr

3. **Photo sharing sites** – Flikr, Instagram, Pinterest, Snapchat

4. **Publishing tools** – WordPress, Wix, Weebly, Google Sites

5. **Rating/Review sites** – Amazon ratings, Angie's List, Yelp

6. **Video sharing sites** – YouTube, Vimeo

7. **Personal broadcasting tools** – Blog Talk Radio, Ustream, Livestream, Blab, Periscope, Facebook Live, Google Hangout

8. **Consultations/Virtual Meetings** – Skype, Join.Me

9. **Location based services** – Foursquare, Yelp

10. **Group buying** – GroupOn, Living Social

11. **Crowdfunding** – Kickstarter, GoFundMe, Indiegogo

CHAPTER 2

DETERMINING YOUR TARGET AUDIENCE

Who are your customers?

Although it seems unrelated, knowing your target audience is one of the success factors for your social media platforms. Before choosing your platforms and creating your content, you must know whom you want to connect.

Think of it like this…when you know who they are, you will know what they want to hear. When they hear the right things, they will follow you. When the right people follow you, they will consume your product or service. That is the simplified formula for getting new business on social media.

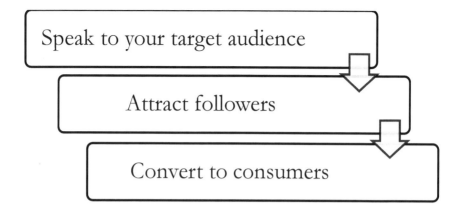

To determine your target audience, here are important factors to consider:

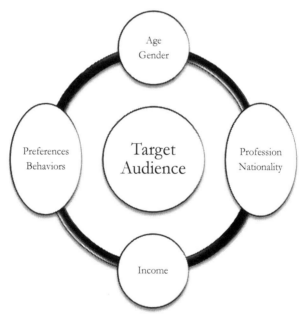

Your target audience is the group of people who will more likely want your product or service. To make that determination, consider demographics such as:

- age
- gender
- income
- profession and nationality
- Psychographics such as their behaviors and preferences (i.e. do they travel, read magazines, enroll in classes, etc.)

Answer these questions:

- Where is your demographic located?
- What are some of their daily habits?
- Do you want to target only women or men as well?
- Is there a particular age group you are looking to target?

Your target audience cannot be EVERYONE. Why? Because it is hard to speak to everyone in the same tone. Youth are addressed differently than senior citizens. Similarly, women respond to different things than men do.

Narrowing your target audience does not mean you will not ever attract anyone outside of that group. It simply means that your marketing efforts are focused on the dominant group you want to reach. A confused mind does not buy nor does it refer, so you want to speak clearly to your audience. Knowing who they are is an important task to fulfill early on.

Example of Target Audience

Clothing Boutique:
Women, 18-35 years old, fashion-oriented, readers of Cosmopolitan & Vogue magazines, attends entertainment and networking events, active in the community.

CHAPTER 3

CHOOSING SOCIAL MEDIA PLATFORMS

Which social media platforms should you use?

The first step when using social media is making sure you have the appropriate platforms created and optimized with all information about yourself and your company. You want to ensure the name is consistent across platforms to be easily found. If the same name is not available across every platform, choose something as close to it as possible. In many instances, it will still come up in the search.

Aim for consistency; consistency builds trust. Let your followers hear from you every day. To be able to manage that, choose two to three platforms to establish your presence. Add more when you can maintain more.

Now that you have identified your target audience, combine that with your marketing goals, and it will be easier for you to know which platforms to be on.

Facebook

Facebook was designed to give you the power to share and to make the world more open and connected. It is excellent for connecting and building relationships. **There are three main options on Facebook:** Personal Page, Public Page, and Groups. All three serve different purposes.

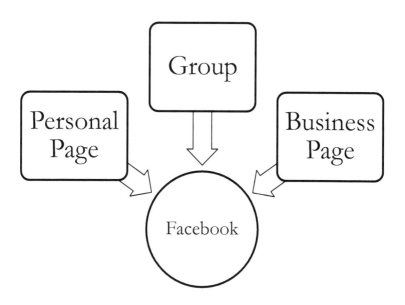

Facebook Personal Page

This is your private space on Facebook where you invite and accept friend requests. These settings can be as private as you choose or as public as you choose. So what does this have to do with business?

People prefer connecting with people. When you meet someone new or reconnect with an old classmate, what is the first thing they do? They go to the 'About' section of your timeline to find out your employment status, relationship status, and all the personal, juicy details that make life interesting. Here is how you tap into that curiosity:

- **Under Work and Education**, add your company name, position, and a brief description outlining what you do.
- **List any professional skills** that are consistent with your profession and industry. For example, a hair stylist may want to list the things she is good at such as coloring, cutting, styling, or caring for natural hair. An event planner may want to list event conception, execution, and décor.
- **Under Contact and Basic Info**, include your website and other social media accounts.

- **Under 'Details About You,'** tell your story including volunteer activities and what inspired you to start your business. That is the perfect transition into talking about the business. You may also use an existing (updated) bio.
- **Make all these fields public.** They can become a pipeline for new business.

Bonus: on your timeline, there is an intro section in the left margin that gives you 101 characters to post. You can be cute and post something fun. Alternatively, you can use it as the gift it is to tell your friends and followers what you do in one powerful sentence. Once you edit that section, be sure to click 'publish to newsfeed.'

Content

Your friend page is your private space and should be used the way you choose. Your choices are:
1. Use this page just for family and friends
2. Use this page to build a network

If you choose option two, your friend list will include people you don't know but would like to get to know. Consider them strangers just for a little while.

Below, I have listed a few suggestions for content. Your final decision on what you choose to post, however, will be based on how comfortable you are sharing publicly with a mixed audience of people you know and do not know.

As a general guideline, your goal is to engage authentically with people socially to build relationships. For the more private person, choose two to three things you are comfortable sharing. For the open, extroverted personality, go for it, but remember that you are branding yourself; everything you post should reflect positively on your brand.

1. Fun stories about your kids or pets
2. Sports
3. Favorite TV Shows (especially the trending ones)
4. Inspirational
5. Updates on your journey in life
6. Projects you're working on (written from a personal perspective versus a business perspective)
7. Community issues
8. Current events
9. Important milestones in life (i.e. graduation, wedding, birth of a baby, etc.)

Frequency

Be active daily. Post a minimum of one time per day. Like and comment on your friends' posts and respond to comments on your posts. Provide an opportunity for others to get to know you. Being engaged and staying engaged will help to open many other doors.

Facebook Groups

Facebook groups are your chance to build a network or community of people around a common interest such as geography, networking, profession, or a hobby. To decide if a group is the right thing to do, answer these questions:

1. What are you trying to accomplish? Building a network or promoting a business?
2. Do you have the time to monitor and maintain the interactions within the community?
3. What ground rules of behavior are you comfortable with? Are members permitted to promote or sell products/services? Are they required to invite other people to join the group?

If a group is the right choice for you:

- include a clear description of the group
- select the most fitting group category
- choose the type of group: open, closed, secret
- attach tags (keywords) that will help your group be found more quickly (providing it is not a secret group)

Content

Content should be driven by the members based on how you define the group as well as the ground rules listed. The group can:

- have free reign to post anything
- post about the topic of the group
- post promotional posts
- post resources and tips in alignment with the group's purpose

Note: there are some groups designed as an extension of a business' services or to provide resources to its group members. In those instances, the group administrator frequently posts as a leader of content and discussion.

Frequency

There should be daily activity in the group. With that type of frequency, the group becomes more beneficial to everyone.

Facebook Public Page

A Facebook Public Page (the page where people click the 'Like' button) is designed primarily for businesses and public figures to promote themselves. Many people think it is better to do their brand building and promotions just from their personal pages.

A public page, however, is public and searchable. The best way to be found online is to be searchable and accessible.

Benefits of a Public Page:

1. **You are more searchable.** When a consumer searches for your name or company name, your public page will show up in the results. Because it is open to everyone, it is easily accessible even to those who do not have Facebook accounts. Viewers can see all the information about your company as well as interactions between you and followers.

2. **Opportunities are earned because of your public page.** The quality of information, number of likes, and engagement with followers influences the decisions of your prospects. Authors have been known to get book deals because of their strong presence. Actors have been known to get the role over someone else; because it is perceived, they can draw a bigger crowd to the production. Your public page matters.

3. **Your presentation is more professional.** The focus is on your product/service, so viewers don't have to sift through all the posts and tags from your friends. It allows you to control the perception, which is important for building a reputable brand.

Your personal page, however, is a permission-based platform. For people to see all the interactions and posts (unless all of your posts are made public), they have to send a friend request and await acceptance. Once accepted, they have to navigate through all of your personal posts to find what they are looking for. **Your online presence should be set up to work for you while you are offline doing other things.**

What is the most effective way to set up your public page?

The 'About' Tab has several fields for you to complete. The available fields depend on the category you choose for your page. Viewers who read this tab have taken a serious interest in your company, which makes it important to focus on. The content you put there is also indexed on Google, which, once again, helps you to be included in search results.

Most fields are self-explanatory but here are a few to pay attention to:

The Ideal Bio (labeled as 'About' on your 'About' tab)

Labeled 'About,' this section appears on your 'About' tab. With only 155 characters available, make it short, clear and to the point. You want people to know exactly what you do or the intent of the page because you have seven seconds to drive home this point.

If you are an author, state clearly that you are an author and the title of your book or the genre of your books.

If you are a ministry, state the denomination and names of your pastors.

If you are a retailer, indicate your merchandise.

If you are a public figure, clearly state what you do (i.e. motivational speaker, pastor, news correspondent, etc.).

You get the picture. Apply this to your particular business line. Include in your 'About' section something that is unique about your brand. Make it your own.

Examples of 'About' statements

Players Preferred offers clothing, art, and accessories inspired by the music, principles, & attitude of the Hip-Hop Culture.

Welcome to The New York Times on Facebook – a hub for conversation about news and ideas. Like our page and connect with Times journalists and readers.

The Breakthrough Specialist, Co-Author Chicken Soup for the Soul, Teacher of The Secret and Author of No Matter What! (Lisa Nichols)

Category

The most important distinction is whether to choose local business. If you are a brick and mortar or an attorney or insurance agent that is licensed only to practice in a particular region, then choose local business. It will ask you to input your hours, parking options, address, and things specific to your location.

If you serve customers and clients around the world on a regular basis, look for a category that fits your function. There are many to choose from such as Brands & Products, People, Sports, Television, Websites & Blogs, and more. Your choice of a category will dictate the fields made available to you to complete the information about your brand.

Story

Use this section as you please, but think of it as an opportunity to connect with your followers. Every business has a story. Consider succinctly telling your followers how your vision came about and the birth of your business. Pulling people into your journey helps to create loyal followers because you have given them something real to connect to.

Contact Info

This is the only section that is clickable. I am a firm believer in the one-click process (or as few clicks as possible) to makes things easier for your followers. So use this section to list your website and other social media accounts. If you do not have a website, type another social media site that you are active on.

Once people like you, they become interested in learning more about you and your business. Make it easy for them to find those other sites.

Note: when selecting the Instagram site, only add your username. Facebook automatically adds the domain name. For example, instead of www.instagram.com/suzyturn, I just added suzyturn. Otherwise, it will not be clickable.

Overall, use the fields to communicate what your brand is about, the list of products/services offered and how they can take advantage of them. If a field is labeled 'awards' or something else and it is not applicable to you, feel free to use it for other types of information. The idea is to make the most important information easy to find and understand.

Cover Photo

The cover photo is the large image at the top of your account. The most important thing to know is the dimension: 851x315. If you use an image of a smaller dimension, it will stretch the photo making it look blurry and granulated. I am sure that is not the first impression you want to make.

The image should reflect your brand. If you have a retail company, your cover photo should reflect high-quality images of your merchandise. If you are an author, your cover photo should reflect your latest book or a collage of your books. You get the idea.

Your cover photo and profile photo are the first things people will see should they choose to visit your page. Invest in getting it professionally designed. Alternatively, you can use a high-resolution professional photo. If you decide to use a professional photo, be sure it is landscape (instead of portrait). Again, think of the type of first impression you want to make. If the images are not high quality, why should they believe that your work or relationship with them would be high quality?

Profile Photo

Let this image be a reflection of your business. It will be attached to every post as a thumbnail image so that it will be continuously associated with your content. You can use a head shot if it is a public figure page or a logo if it is a traditional business page.

This image is a perfect square (170x170), so if your logo is a horizontal image, it may not fit very well there. Your options are to get another image designed or use a professional photo that depicts what your business is about (i.e. merchandise, models, product, etc.).

Content

This platform is strictly for the purposes of business, so it is not the ideal place to regularly post about family functions, and fun kid stories unless it is relevant to the page's mission. Your starting point is thinking of how you can offer value to your audience. Be audience focused. Below are suggestions (see a detailed list toward the end):

1. Tips and advice
2. Answering frequently asked questions
3. Behind the scenes footage (i.e. an event, planning process, snippet of a meeting, etc.)
4. Explanation of products and services

Answer this question: How can you give your followers a taste of the experience, value, and quality you have to offer?

Frequency

Post two to three times per day. The worst-case scenario is once per day for the sake of consistency, but it is best to post at least two to three times daily.

LinkedIn

With more than 467 million users (Source: expandedrambling.com), LinkedIn is the world's largest professional social network in the world of social media. It is designed to be a networking tool for professional purposes as opposed to social purposes. Regardless of your profession, it is recommended that every person creates a LinkedIn account and keep it updated.

When used the right way, it can become your electronic Rolodex. You learn more about your connections in five minutes than if you met them in person. Why? Because it is the only platform where you can comprehensively present your professional background and expertise.

3 Top Ways LinkedIn is Used

1. **LinkedIn is used by professionals as a branding and accessibility tool.** Business owners and professionals create profiles that present them as credible experts in their respective industries. It becomes a marketing tool that when used effectively attracts the right viewers. The more active you are on LinkedIn, the more your profile is noticed and viewed. LinkedIn rewards activity.

2. **B2B (business-to-business) marketers have great success on LinkedIn.** When your customers are businesses, LinkedIn provides a more valuable network than any other social media platform. Forty-five percent of LinkedIn members are upper management executives, which is typically the group that makes the decisions (Source: B2bnn.com). LinkedIn is also known for generating more leads than other social networks including Facebook (Source: B2bnn.com).

   Almost 50 percent of recruiters use LinkedIn to find candidates (Source: ExpandedRamblings.com). Ninety-four percent use LinkedIn to research and evaluate candidates (Source: ExpandedRamblings.com).

3. With robust professional information available, recruiters simply have to sift through to find candidates that meet their criteria. This is another reason it is important to present a strong, comprehensive profile.

What is the most effective way to set up your LinkedIn profile?

Profile Strength

All-Star

Be as comprehensive as you can when completing your profile. LinkedIn displays a graphic that shows your progress of completion. It is best to complete every field made available. As a professional, you want to provide enough information to recruiters to decide whether you are a potential candidate.

As a business owner or freelance consultant, you want to provide potential clients with enough data to determine that you are credible and knowledgeable in your industry. Remember, you want your online presence to work in your favor while you are offline taking care of business. When there is insufficient data, you may not have another opportunity to make a good impression. Engagement is hard to regain, so capture it while you can.

Here are some important fields to pay attention to:

Professional Photo

Add a professional photo. I stress the word 'professional' and 'selfie' or photo taken with a mobile device is not considered a professional photo. A photo taken at a party, no matter how nice you looked that night, is not a professional photo. A photo with the mall in the background is not a professional photo.

If you want to be taken seriously, invest in yourself by hiring a professional photographer or going to a department store like JCPenny that offers photography services. You are likely to be found 14 times more than usual when you have a professional photo (Source: ExpandedRamblings.com).

Professional Headline

LinkedIn allows you to include a statement that classifies who you are as a professional. In 120 characters or less, be clear about what you do and the benefit you offer. My professional headline reads: Increasing Online Visibility for Small Businesses & Public Figures. Be sure your headline is specific, and value added.

Volunteering Opportunities

Demonstrating that you volunteer your time to help others presents you in a positive light. Giving back is important to most, if not all, companies. It also shows additional dimensions and expertise beyond your professional background. Think of it as an opportunity to separate yourself from the competition as well as establish common ground between you and important connections. Breaking the ice is easier when you have something in common.

Additional Categories

LinkedIn lists many other categories that allow you to shine light on your many accomplishments such as awards, projects, courses, patents, and publications. Each of these categories allows you to present another notch in your belt that can give you the edge you need to be selected for a new job or new client. If a field does not apply to you, leave it blank. It will not work against you.

The Ideal Summary

Think of this section as a bio. However, make it a little more personal and interactive. You have 2,000 characters to tell a short story about who you are and what you offer. The most important thing to keep in mind is that you control this platform, so present the information in a way that molds the readers' perception of you. Portray yourself the way you want to be seen and include whatever you think is important. Many times, people read the summary or conclusion first, because they give the most complete picture.

Skills

LinkedIn provides a library of skills to choose from. Select those that show the breadth of your capabilities. However, be sure your skills support your professional headline and the role you want to be known for. If you have strong administrative assistant skills, but you want to be seen as a manager, those skills are no longer relevant. As you connect with people you know, they will endorse the skills they most associate you with.

Professional Experience

Do not feel compelled to list your entire professional background. Think of how you want to be branded. If the first five years of your career was administrative or in fast food and the last five years were in higher-level positions, which is the direction of your career path, only list the last five years. Remember, you control your platforms. These are not legally binding documents although it is important to be truthful and authentic.

Recommendations

Online recommendations are considered social proof. It dramatically increases your credibility. When building your network, you want to add new people. That means you (and your work) are a stranger to that new connection. You cut through a lot of the skepticism when there are recommendations readily available.

To request a recommendation, follow these steps:
1. Click on down arrow next to 'Me' in the top navigation bar
2. Select 'view profile.'
3. Scroll down to the recommendations section
4. Click on the pencil next to 'Ask to be recommended' and follow the prompts
5. Click on 'Ask for a recommendation' and follow the prompts

I also suggest you send an email or call the person you have sent the recommendation request to and ask that it be completed by your preferred date. Do not leave it open ended.

Groups

Another important LinkedIn feature is groups. Groups are community forums created by LinkedIn members; anyone can create a group. You will find them organized by industry, subject matter, etc. Find the ones applicable to you and join. It is an easier way to navigate the millions of people on LinkedIn and get connected with the right people. Being active in groups is also another way to get exposure for yourself and your business. If you have a blog, this is a perfect place to post it.

Bonus Tip: Create a custom URL for your account. It makes it easier to direct people there.

1. Click the down arrow next to 'Me' on the navigation bar.
2. Select view profile.
3. In the right margin, click on 'edit public profile.'
4. It will take you to another screen. In the top right column, click on the pencil beneath edit public profile URL.
5. Type in a custom extension. I recommend your name or some variation of it.

Note: from LinkedIn: Your custom URL must contain 5-30 letters or numbers. Please do not use spaces, symbols, or special characters.

Be active

Just like on Facebook, you can post on your profile. It will be seen in the newsfeed of your network. Keep in mind that this is a professional network, so stick to anything that brands you according to your position and industry.

While articles tend to fail miserably on Facebook, they do very well on LinkedIn. Sixty-seven percent of LinkedIn users consider themselves news junkies (Source:

ExpandedRambling.com). When you post, you increase the number of your profile views. It pays off!

Content

Just a reminder that this is a professional network. Every post brands you professionally. Since LinkedIn is a news junkie platform, see some content suggestions below:

- Articles and resources in your industry
- Breaking news in your industry
- Blogs you have written
- Tips and advice in your field

Answer these questions:

How do you want people to view you professionally? What do you want them to think of you?

Frequency

Post a status update at least once per day. It will draw attention to your profile. Comment and interact with the posts of your connections on your timeline and in groups daily. Relationship building is important. It also allows people to see you in a different light, which helps to move the relationship to a deeper level.

Fun fact:

Microsoft purchased LinkedIn in a $26.2 billion all-cash deal. Currently, the plan is for LinkedIn and its culture to remain intact. The restructuring of the site has already begun but are intended to make the user experience better.

Twitter

Twitter is an often misunderstood and feared platform. However, there is tremendous value in it. Referred to as a micro-blogging platform by many, Twitter is a social network where each tweet (defined as a post) is 140 characters. Some think that's not enough, but that is the fun in it.

It is also at the forefront of releasing breaking news around the world before major news networks and has become a go-to source internationally for communicating during world crises. Because of its ease in communicating, many businesses such as airlines, technology companies, and online retail businesses use it for customer service purposes.

Surprising audiences that frequent Twitter includes:
- Senior Executives
- Celebrities
- Teens
- Men

The added bonus is that it is much easier to connect with someone of influence on Twitter than any other platform. They are more responsive because there is less clutter to sift through.

Bonus Tip: Twitter allows you to include a link or attach a photo, 30-second maximum video, or GIF file to your tweet. Currently, it takes away from the 140 characters. With the recent Twitter changes, media attachments (i.e. photos, videos, and gifs) no longer affect the 140 characters.

Here are some important terms to be aware of:

- **Tweet:** your 140 characters or less post is called a tweet (*what NOT to say:* I sent you a twitter or I twittered).
- **Retweet:** reposting or sharing a tweet.
- **Hashtag:** Hashtags are now popular on most social media platforms. It is the # sign with a word or string of words attached.
- **Handle:** your username. For example, my handle is @suzyturn.
- **Direct Message (DM):** Sending a private message to someone, similar to Facebook Messenger. However, you can only DM someone who is following you.
- **Reply:** responding with a comment to someone's tweet.

- **@:** insert this character before a person's username, and it tags them, also known as a mention. It is a public way to send someone a message.
- **Home:** that is your newsfeed page showing tweets from everyone you are following.
- **Me:** that is your timeline showing only your posts. You will see this option on your mobile device.
- **Moments:** a collection of the biggest stories trending in the news.
- **Notifications:** anything that involves your account or any activity you are involved in will be here. It is a chance for you to catch up on what you missed.

To set up your account, complete these important sections:

Name/Username

There are two fields for names: (1) full name or company name and (2) username (also known as your handle).

Suzzette Turnbull
@suzy4um

- If your Twitter account brands you, use your full name in the name field. If it brands your company, use your company name. This field has a

20-character limit. Twitter also prohibits users from including these words: Twitter or Admin.

- For your handle/username, there is a 15-character limit, and it is written as one word (no spaces but underscore allowed). This handle also becomes a part of your Twitter custom link, which is automatically assigned to you. For example, my twitter link is https://twitter.com/suzyturn www.twitter.com/suzyturn.

- Keep in mind that if you decide to change your handle, which you can do at any time, it must also be changed anywhere else you have it listed or linked to. Otherwise, it will lead people to the wrong account.

- *Note:* whatever you choose brands you, so be sure your handle is one that gives people the impression you want them to have (if you decide to use something different than your name).

- If the name or handle you had in mind exceeds the number of characters available, think of something that is the next closest choice. You may have to abbreviate parts of it. Be sure it is easy to remember and relevant to your brand. Here is a **bad example**: @15793book or @smsklg. That may have significance to the user but will be confusing to your audience (and hard to remember).

The Ideal Bio

Your Twitter bio has 160 characters available. Use it to clearly state what you offer or who you are (i.e. author, speaker, etc.). While your parenting roles and other fun things in your life may be important to you, lead with your business contributions if that is your purpose for using Twitter. You have seven seconds to convince that potential follower to click the follow button.

Do not include a website address; there is a separate field for that. The exception to this is if you would like to include more than one website address for promotional reasons.

Profile Photo

If the account brands you, use a current professional photo. People like to connect with people so put a face with your name. It is a great connection point. The dimension is 400x400.

If it brands your business, use a professionally designed logo. If it brands a show, book, or something of that sort, use an image that reflects that. Once again, it gives people another connection point.

Cover Photo

The cover photo is the large image at the top of your account. The most important thing to know is the dimension: 1500x500. If you use an image of a smaller dimension, it will stretch the photo making it look blurry and granulated. I am sure that is not the first impression you want to make.

The image should reflect your brand. If you have a retail company, your cover photo should reflect high-quality images of your merchandise. If you are an author, your cover photo should reflect your latest book or a collage of your books. You get the idea.

Your cover photo and profile photo are the first things people will see. Invest in getting it professionally designed. Alternatively, you can use a high-resolution professional photo. Again, think of the type of the first impression you want to make. If the images are not high quality, why should they think your work or relationship with them would be high quality?

Website

Use the website address that drives people to where you want them to learn more about you or connect with you next. It should be a part of your marketing and engagement strategy. Keep in mind that if you do not have a blog or subscribe features set up on your website, sending them there means they will read the information, leave, and probably not return.

Examples of sites to direct them to include:
- A traditional website
- A Facebook page
- SoundCloud (if you're an artist or speaker)
- YouTube
- eCommerce site

Content

Like Facebook, Twitter is active socially. There is a lot of conversation and engagement taking place. Celebrities and public figures often air their grievances between one another on Twitter as well. However, it is also filled with news junkies. Finally, yet importantly, there are many customer complaints communicated and resolved via Twitter.

Below are some suggestions for content:
- Articles and resources
- Industry news
- Industry tips and advice
- Recommendation of resources
- Your perspective on industry news
- Inspiration
- Company policies serving to assist customers with issues (i.e. Call or email us with any issue you are experiencing. We are here to help.)

Frequency

To maximize Twitter, tweet a minimum of five times per day, which does not include responses. Be active in responding to tweets where you are mentioned (found in your notifications) and replying to tweets of those, you are following. When responding, you can respond to those things you personally enjoy like replying to a sports commentator or your favorite author.

Instagram

Instagram was designed for you to show followers the world through your eyes. It is an image (photo or video) driven social network that can be categorized as a microblogging site which has made it quite popular with more than 600 million users surpassing Twitter. Because it is image driven, good quality photos are important. Businesses and public figures that can tell their story or present their brand easily using images do very well on Instagram.

A fun fact: Facebook owns Instagram. Instagram is much easier to set up than other social networks.

Here are important fields to pay attention to:

Names
Similar to Twitter, there are two name fields to complete: (1) full name or company name and (2) username. The most important thing to know is that both fields are searchable (meaning they will come up in search engine or Instagram searches).

When you enter into 'edit profile' mode, **the top field** allows you to enter a traditional name – your given name, your business name, etc. I highly recommend you use this field to reflect the name that is on your business card and that you use legally. Or if this account is for your business, use the name of your business.

Think of it like this. How do you introduce yourself when you go to a networking event? Do you introduce yourself using your given name or your nickname? Most people use their given name. Providing you have made a good impression, after the event, people will look for you on social media by your given name. Your ultimate goal is to be found so you can continue building those connections.

The exception to this rule is an entertainer or public figure that has a stage name. Naturally, your stage name will function as your given name because that is how your followers know you.

The second field is where you create a username. It must be unique (meaning no one else is using it), and it is limited to 30 characters. The permissible characters are letters, numbers, periods, and underscores. You have an opportunity to have some fun here; you may have to be creative if your original choice is unavailable. However, keep in mind that you are still branding yourself. How do you want people to perceive you? Let that be your guide.

The Ideal Bio

The bio field is limited to 150 characters. Be succinct and clear in making sure people know what you do and what you offer. If you are using this for business reasons, lead with your business offerings and focus. You can also add emojis, which is a fun element. Instagram gives the opportunity for your creativity to shine through.

The bio section does not allow you to do hard returns, but if you choose to include hard returns, type your bio in your notes app, then copy and paste into your bio section.

Example of Bio:

Account name: Happy Wife Life
Username: thewifecoach
Bio: "All Married Women Aren't Wives." The Wife Coach educates, prepares, & coaches women BEFORE & AFTER they say "I Do." Happy marriages begin with YOU!

(*Note:* this works well when she leads with 'thewifecoach' at events, so she is easily found.)

Website

The most important thing to know is that this is **THE ONLY** place (at this time) you will find a clickable link on Instagram. The great thing about this field is that you can change it as often as you would like. Be sure to make it consistent with your marketing strategy. **Here are some possible uses for this field:**

If you have an event, include the link to register for the event.

If you have just released a book, include a link to purchase the book.

If you are a blogger, include the blog link for each blog as it is released.

If you have an e-commerce site, include a link for people to shop.

If you have a special offer, include a link directly to that offer.

If you have a gallery of photos that support new photography services or modeling services, include a link directly to the gallery.

If you are an actor, include a link directly to your acting reel.

In between major activities, drive people to your website or Facebook page.

Whatever you are promoting during a particular season in your business, be sure your link supports that. When you post, direct people to click the link in your bio as the call to action.

Bonus Tip: You can be logged into more than one Instagram account at one time. Why is that important? Some people have a personal account and a business account. Alternatively, maybe they work full-time jobs while pursuing their own entrepreneurial ventures. It is a convenient feature.

Content

Instagram is ideal for businesses and public figures who can easily translate what they do using pictures or video. If you are not an image driven business or do not lead an image driven public figure lifestyle (such as a celebrity), create an image quote (you will see app recommendations for this later) or use an image that conveys the sentiment of your post. For example, many social media experts create images that display the tip or point being made.

Here are some content suggestions:

- Quotes/Inspiration
- Scriptures
- Fashion
- Attending events
- Your product (i.e. homes for realtors, pictures of work for photographers, styled customers for hair stylists and make-up artists, paintings for artists, culinary dishes for chefs, etc.)
- Ingredients or supplies used for your craft

- Resources (i.e. recommended book – use the book cover or pages of the book)
- Promotional images (i.e. event, book, webinar, etc.)
- Happy customers
- Repost positive posts about your brand by other Instagram users

Instagram has added a feature that allows you to post multiple photos and videos in one post (up to 10). I have not found that this feature increases engagement; however, it is a cool addition that helps to:

- tell a story by showing various aspects of a situation or event
- show before and after transformations
- show multiple speakers or performers for an event
- and more

Note: these ideas can also be used on Facebook in addition to the previous suggestions. Be sure your content choices tie into your brand.

Frequency

Ideally, do two to three posts per day. Some say one post per day is all that is needed and with the right set of hashtags that post will work for days. However, to keep your followers engaged, more than one post is important.

Periscope

Periscope is one of the newer social media platforms and provides an international live video broadcast experience from your phone where the user controls the settings. It provides a great touch point by giving your followers a real-time encounter. Feedback from people watching live broadcasts remotely is that they feel like they are there in person. Periscope also provides a map that allows users to join any live Periscope around the world so you can spread your wings and travel virtually. **Fun fact:** Periscope is owned by Twitter.

Creating an Account/Logging In

There are two ways to get started. Either use your Twitter login information or use your phone number. I recommend using your Twitter login information. Be logged into Twitter before logging into Periscope. It makes it easier. If you are logged into multiple accounts, select the Twitter account consistent with the Periscope account you are creating.

Once both accounts are connected, when you go live on Periscope, a tweet is automatically sent out through your Twitter account. That expands the reach of your invitation to join the Periscope broadcast.

If you do not have a Twitter account, create one before getting started on Periscope (see the Twitter section above for details). It helps you to grow your presence.

If you feel strongly that you do not want to have a Twitter account, create the account with your phone number from the phone you want to use Periscope on (Don't worry; Periscope will not stalk you. Your number is only used for the purposes of logging in). Expect an SMS (text message) with a confirmation code.

Bio and Username

When you log in with your Twitter account, your bio, name, and username will automatically transfer to your Periscope account. You will see an 'edit' option in the top right of your profile screen so feel free to make edits. Your followers and people you are following on Twitter will not transfer, however.

When logging in with a phone number, your username must be two or more characters. The bio is limited to 160 characters, but it will display up to 122 characters followed by several dots. Unlike Twitter, there isn't a separate field for a website. Feel free to edit your profile and add a website within the 122 characters if this is important to your marketing strategy.

Bonus Tip: You can save your broadcast to your camera roll. After you stop the broadcast, scroll down, and you will see the option. Sometimes it takes a few seconds, but this must be done before you close the app. If you know that, you will be saving all periscopes, go to your settings, and select 'auto-save to camera roll.' To be able to re-use this video (on Instagram, Facebook, etc.), you must have periscoped with the phone upright versus sideways.

Bonus Bonus Tip: Periscope has changed the expiration timeframe on its videos. The default is now for videos to remain permanently. You still have the option to change it to expire after 24 hours if you choose.

Content

Brand related Periscopes do much better. It is more of a substantive platform than a social platform, so choose topics that relate to what your product or service delivers.

- Sound off on industry news (people love the dialogue on Periscope)
- Tips and advice

- Frequently asked questions that are industry related (i.e. a dentist can discuss the benefits of flossing and the preferred brands of floss to use)
- Hot, trending topics that are industry related
- Take burning questions from followers and find out what else they want to know about
- Behind the scenes footage (i.e. events, movie sets, stage plays, etc.)
- Inspiration/Spiritual Motivation/Prayer

Frequency

Daily activity is ideal, but if you are unable to do that, plans to be active at least three times per week. There is a lot of spontaneity in using Periscope, so if you know that you have some Periscope worthy activities coming up, that will help with your engagement.

Here are a few schedules people use:

- Some users have a set day and time that is communicated to their followers on all platforms. It's like a weekly event. Then the other Periscopes are spontaneous.
- Others communicate a set time that they log on daily.

- Others do all Periscopes spontaneously since all followers are notified.

The choice is yours based on what you will maintain, but two to three times per week is important.

Pinterest

With more than 175 million monthly active users, Pinterest is more of a niche account versus for the masses like Facebook. It's considered a content sharing platform where users share pictures of their 'favorites' – favorite recipes, favorite shoes, favorite quotes, favorite event décor and more.

This greatly benefits businesses because these 'favorites' are being shared from your websites or being re-pinned from your Pinterest account.

The user experience is like flipping through a catalog making it somewhat of a search engine. Just like users use Google and YouTube to find information, they are using Pinterest as well. This makes the quality of the photos very important. *Note:* a pin is a post on Pinterest.

How does it benefit users?

It links back to the source of the photo providing the source was a website. For example, if you pin from your website, it becomes like a trail that leads viewers back to your site. Imagine if you're a food blogger. You naturally include photos of your dishes in your blog. Pinning those photos will lead viewers back to read and possibly subscribe to your blog.

Who is (and should be) using Pinterest for business?

- Event planners (i.e. wedding planners, social event planners, etc.)
- Retailers (i.e. products, merchandise, fashion, jewelry, etc.)
- Make-up artists
- Photographers
- Fashion stylists and blogs
- Hairstylists
- Magazines that are image driven
- Chefs
- Food establishments (i.e. restaurants, fast food, food trucks, food providers, supermarkets, etc.)
- Food and beverage brands (i.e. Nabisco, Grey Goose, etc.)
- Blog and social media experts
- And any company that can showcase their products or services using photos

How does Pinterest work?

Users create boards, and each board has a name. All boards created should collectively tell the story of your brand. For example, if you are a wedding planner, here are some boards you may want to create in order to become a one-stop-shop for brides. By the way, Pinterest has become a great source of information for brides, grooms, and wedding planners.

- Wedding venues
- Wedding destinations
- Honeymoon destinations
- Wedding dresses
- Bridesmaid dresses
- Groom and groomsmen tuxes
- Wedding cakes
- Bridal shower décor and themes
- Wedding themes and color schemes
- Wedding gift ideas
- You get the idea…

Here are some fields to pay attention to when creating your account:

Account Name

This field is for your name or business name and is limited to 38 characters. Use the name that people associate you or your business with.

Username

Pinterest usernames have a limit of three to 15 characters. Like other usernames, it is listed as one word, no spaces. Keep in mind how you want to be branded. Do your best to use the same username across all platforms or come as close to it as possible.

Picture

Use a professional picture if the account brands you. If it brands your business, use a professionally designed logo.

The Ideal Bio

The About You section is limited to 160 characters. Be sure to explain clearly, who you are and what you offer. Feel free to use your Instagram bio and Facebook page's short description. It is important to have consistency across platforms. Keep in mind that search engines pull from this information so connect it to your industry and the search terms that will help you to be found.

Website

There is a separate field for your website, so it isn't necessary to include it in your bio. Once you have inputted your website, be sure to take the extra step to verify it. Once you have confirmed that you or your business owns the account, you will get a check next to your website, which will also give, you access to Pinterest analytics. Analytics allows you to see the traffic coming to your site from Pinterest.

Content

Pinterest is another image driven site. The difference between Pinterest and Instagram is that Pinterest is not intended to include social conversation. It's about sharing photos of your favorite things or those things important to you. In your case, photos related to your brand that other users enjoy and would be interested in.

Here are some ideas of images to showcase:

- Event décor
- Culinary dishes (showcases recipes)
- Savory beverages (showcases liqueur and drink recipes)
- Photography samples reflective of a photographer's services and specialties
- Hairstyles
- You get the picture…

Frequency

Be active at least once per day to keep your brand in users' streams. Keep in mind that users also search by subject matter, so one of your goals is to come up in searches with current and relevant information.

Snapchat

Snapchat is the newest fascination among teens and young adults. They are enthralled by the instantaneous nature of this platform and the face-to-face chat feeling it inspires. Another feature they find to be an advantage is the 24-hour expiration of all snaps as well as the ability to create a "story" for their feed or to send directly to select friends.

It also comes with a host of features, which you have probably seen like geofilters, which adds animal ears and noses (and other creative images) to your photos. Snapchat entices users with their slogan, "Life's more fun when you live it in the moment." Their features are conducive to that slogan which includes a max 10-second video feature.

If you have a youth audience, it is critical that you create a snapchat account and use it often. Youth are primarily found on Snapchat, Twitter, and some on Instagram.

Setting up Snapchat is very simple and has the least amount of steps of all the platforms. Another reason youth love it…the simplicity of it.

Username

Create a username that is unique. The edit name field gives you a 30-character limit. Remember that you want to be found and identified by this username, so make it consistent with your other platforms.

Profile Picture

This is a fun platform so feel free to use a fun picture. Snapchat allows you to take a selfie from the app if you choose. Although it is fun, always keep your branding in mind and be sure you are appropriately groomed for the selfie.

Who is using Snapchat?

- Celebrities
- Award Shows like Tony Awards
- Major events like Coachella
- News networks like CNN
- Online Radio like iHeartRadio
- Magazines like People Magazine and Cosmopolitan
- Social Media Outlets like Mashable
- Online News Platforms like BuzzFeed
- Sports News like ESPN
- Television Networks like the Food Network
- And so much more….everyone is jumping on to Snapchat

Bonus Tip: Snapchat is the platform where people feel incredibly liberated and allow others to come a little further into their personal life. Although it's focused on fun, remember that every post creates a digital footprint. Keep your brand in mind. Not everything is meant to be shared on social media. Understand how you want it to fit into your marketing strategy that synchronizes with the culture of the platform.

Content

Think of Snapchat like a Snapdiary. You can chronicle what is happening, and it's acceptable. Use it to capture the journey of whatever is happening in your business or public figure lifestyle. However, keep your brand and reputation in mind.

Frequency

Because this platform is so fast moving, be active daily.

Google+

Google+ is Google's social network. The goal of this network is to recreate your offline interactions. Similar to other social networks, you have the capability to share information with others through your posts and newsfeed. Google+, however, features circles, which is the main distinction; users add people they are following to user created circles. Circles are organized based on user preferences – i.e. family, friends, business acquaintances, foodies, etc. – allowing you to choose who you share posts with along with an option to make your posts public.

Google+ also offers Hangouts, a video chat feature for up to 10 of your connections. You control the privacy of it, but it is ideal for meetings, consultations, study groups, discussions and more.

Google+ has the option to create a regular user page or a business page (*note:* to create a business page, you must have a user account). On a user account, you will have personal fields such as work, education, and basic information.

A business page will ask you to choose a category for the business and to complete fields such as website, contact information and the about field.

Nuance: Google comes with a suite of products, which uses the same account name across all platforms (i.e. YouTube, Google+, and Gmail). Once you log into your Gmail account, you can access the other platforms.

Here are a few fields to keep in mind:

Business Page

Cover Photo

The recommended cover photo dimension is 1080x608. Get it designed professionally or use a high-resolution photo that depicts your business.

In my experience, this dimension is tricky. Leave $1/8^{th}$ of an inch border leeway in your design.

Profile Photo

The profile photo is circular with a dimension of 250x250.

Location

It enhances your searchability when you include a physical location for your business. Even if it is a mailbox address you use for a service-based business, it still gives a sense of where you are located.

The Ideal Tagline

Each business page is allotted 140 characters to add a tagline as a part of its profile. Use it to communicate succinctly what your business does.

The Ideal Company Bio

Clearly, explain what your business is about and demonstrate how you differ from your competitors. What is your competitive advantage or secret sauce (i.e. customer service, experience, expertise, etc.)?

Content

Think of Google+ as you would Facebook. It is a similar set up regarding the essentials of how to post a status update. This platform is strictly for the purposes of business, so it is not the ideal place to regularly post about family functions and fun kid stories unless you create a personal account (the exception is when you create a circle just for your family and friends in order to compartmentalize your personal posts). Your starting point is thinking of how you can offer value to your audience. Be audience focused. Below are suggestions:

1. Tips and advice
2. Answering frequently asked questions
3. Behind the scenes footage (i.e. an event, planning process, snippet of a meeting, etc.)
5. Explanation of products and services
6. Your business or brand related blog (or vlog: video blog)

Answer this question: How can you give your followers a taste of the experience, value, and quality you have to offer?

Frequency

Post two to three times per day. The worst-case scenario is once per day for the sake of consistency, but it is best to post at least two to three times daily.

Yelp

Yelp has become one of the 'go-to' platforms for business reviews. Initially, it became popular for restaurant reviews (and still is), but other local businesses have gotten in on the action as well. Users create an account and can write reviews on any business of their choice.

When creating a user account, Yelp asks personal questions such as your favorite movie, book you're reading, and first concert. Although known as a great source of reviews, it is also a social network where you can make friends and create a custom URL.

Business Page

To set up a business page, scroll to the bottom of the home page and select the 'Claim Your Business Page' option. You will be prompted to find your business before beginning the setup process. Yelp wants to confirm that the business exists. If your business is not found, you will have to add it.

Yelp allows you to add menus, set up a reservation system, add photos, provide check-in offers and more. Take full advantage.

If you are a brick and mortar business, it is important to have a Yelp business account. After servicing each customer, ask them to leave a review for you. Social proof (proof posted online by users) sets you apart from your competition. Potential customers value what customers have to say about your business.

Who is using Yelp?

- Law Firms
- Doctors
- Restaurants
- Retailers
- Nightlife and Entertainment
- Hotels
- Plumbers
- Realtors
- And more...

Bonus Tip: Yelp has a section for submitting events for promotions. I have promoted at least ten events with this feature. If people are already frequenting this platform for information, why not use their free feature to spread the word about an event.

Content

Keep your list of products, services, and specials updated. It's easy to forget about this platform once it has been set up.

- Up to date photos of your products
- Restaurants: continuous pictures of your culinary dishes. Some can be taken with a mobile device

to keep the platform current. Photos with customers who consent to have their picture taken and used publicly.

- Service-based organizations: post pictures (candid and posed) with clients who have provided consent to be in photos.

Frequency

Assign someone to check the platform daily to stay on top of customer feedback. Aside from that, keep things up to date so that potential customers and clients will have relevant data to use in making their decisions.

CHAPTER 4

STREAMLINING POSTS

Some of the social media platforms have options to send your post to other platforms. While this is a convenient feature, it isn't always recommended. For example, Instagram gives you the option to push out to Facebook, Twitter, Tumblr, Flickr, and Swarm.

When making the decision whether to use these features or not, consider the culture of the platform you are pushing out to as a general guideline. In more instances than not, people on Twitter don't like to click on a link to get more information. They enjoy the culture of getting what they need from a tweet in 140 characters. When a post from another platform pushes out to Twitter, and it exceeds 140 characters, Twitter converts the excess into a link. Most followers won't click on a link. That affects your engagement. Exceptions are tweets from celebrities or other well sought after brands.

As another general guideline, look at how the post translates to the other platform. For example, when you push from Instagram to Facebook, if you have mentioned anyone in the caption, it will appear the same way (@whoeverthepersonsnameis). That looks weird on Facebook because that is not the norm. Because I care about my branding, I post to Instagram, then go back and share the post to Facebook. That process allows me to make any edits I want to make. It's an extra step, but it only takes a few seconds.

Instagram → Twitter → Not a good idea
Facebook → Twitter → Not a good idea
Twitter → Facebook → Not a good idea

Bonus Tip: you can push from Instagram to your Facebook public page instead of your personal page. You must first adjust the "Linked Account" settings. *Note:* you cannot do both at the same time. You have to adjust the settings each time you want it to go to a different Facebook location. However, if you have converted your Instagram account to a business account, you can only publish to your Facebook public page.

CHAPTER 5

MONITORING AND MANAGEMENT TOOLS

Monitoring and management tools help users to juggle multiple platforms. Many people ask me if they should be using these platforms. I don't recommend it for everyone, but they are useful tools when you're managing multiple platforms, and you have decided to post the same exact thing on every platform (another thing I don't recommend).

BENEFITS (BASED ON EACH PLATFORM AND PLAN):
- ✓ Log into one platform to access your accounts.
- ✓ Schedule your posts for the various accounts.
- ✓ Keep up with the activity on your accounts.
- ✓ Monitor what people are saying about your brand and industry.
- ✓ Keep the information in one place.
- ✓ View your newsfeeds from the dashboards.

- ✓ Set up the streams in your dashboard the way you choose.
- ✓ Add team members, communicate with them, manage them, and assign tasks (available with paid plans).
- ✓ View analytics. Analytics tell you how much engagement you have, how many new likes, and other measurements of that nature so that you can gauge your effectiveness.
- ✓ If this list overwhelms you, a management tool may not be necessary for you.

Note:

Set aside time every day to check the activity on all your platforms and engage with your audience. Don't set it and forget it.

Here is a basic overview of a few of the most popular management tools (in no particular order):

- **Hootsuite** allows you to connect to Facebook, Twitter, LinkedIn, WordPress, Google+, YouTube, and Instagram by default. Other apps are available for a monthly fee. *Note:* there are some limitations with the free option below.

  - o The **free option** is designed for the individual; it allows one user, up to three accounts (i.e.

Facebook, etc.) and has basic features that include analytics and scheduling posts.

o The **pro option** is designed for entrepreneurs, owners, and consultants for $9.99 per month, up to 10 users and up to 50 social accounts along with a few extra bells and whistles including access to premium apps. If you have a small social media department, social media staff, or volunteers, this is a good option for maximum control. They will not need username and passwords to each platform they are posting on. **There is currently a free 30-day trial for this option.**

o The **business option** is designed for small businesses and agencies that have very established social media departments and efforts. There is no price tag listed; contact must be made with Hootsuite to get started with this option.

• Buffer is known as a simple, easy to use platform for social media management. You can connect Facebook, Twitter, LinkedIn, Google+, and Pinterest. Along with the usual social media management features, it includes an image creator option as well as a tool that helps you select the optimal time to post. The pricing options are a little different.

- o The **Individual Plan** is free and lets you connect one social profile (account) per platform (i.e. Facebook, etc.) and ten scheduled posts per profile. This plan doesn't include Pinterest.

- o The **Awesome Plan** is $10 per month for up to 10 social profiles with 100 scheduled posts per profile. You can try it free for seven days.

- o The **Small Plan** is $99 per month for up to 25 social profiles, five additional team members, and 2,000 scheduled posts per profile. A 30-day free trial is available.

- o The **Medium Plan** is $199 per month for up to 50 social profiles, ten additional team members, and 2,000 scheduled posts per profile. A 30-day free trial is available.

- o The **Large Plan** is $399 per month for up to 150 social profiles, 25 additional team members, and 2,000 scheduled posts per profile. A 30-day free trial is available.

- **SproutSocial** is a paid platform with various pricing options, none of which is free. However, all pricing options provide a 30-day free trial (no credit card required). Although the prices are higher than Hootsuite, SproutSocial offers more functionality. For example, the clean-up feature lets you unfollow accounts that have no activity to help you have quality connections. SproutSocial also gives you assistance with publishing posts at times most likely for your audience to see it.

How do you know if SproutSocial is for you? It's a robust platform, but be aware of its limitations. They may or may not affect you. SproutSocial connects Facebook, Twitter, LinkedIn, Instagram, and Google+ although not every feature is available for all those platforms. If you're on Pinterest, YouTube or other platforms that you want to add, the option isn't available.

- o The Deluxe option is $59 per user per month which includes up to 5 profiles
- o The Premium option is $99 per user per month which includes up to 10 profiles
- o The Enterprise option is $249 per month which includes up to 50 profiles

CHAPTER 6

IMAGE CREATION APPS AND PLATFORMS

Images are the number one viewed media on social media. Adding an image draws the attention of more people than a post with no image or video attached. You have probably been wondering how to make those image quotes and memes. While there are many options, below are several apps and platforms to help you do so easily.

Apps

- Word Swag – available for $3.99 (one-time fee – worth it). Select the Tiffany green image that says Word Swag.
- Word Dream – free. Select the black image that says Word Dream.
- Typorama – free but available on the iPhone only. Select the red image with a capital T.

- Textgram – free. Select the tan image with text gram in lower case cursive with a pencil.
- PhotoGrid – free. This is a photo collage app, but you can also use it to add text to your image. Select the four quadrants, multi-color app (green, yellow, red, and blue).

Image Creator Platforms

- **Canva** (www.canva.com) – an easy to use design platform. Canva provides templates of different sizes for your online use that you add text to. Dimensions include Instagram, Facebook cover photo, presentation, postcard, flyer, invitations and more. The finished product has a professional look.
  - Canva has a free plan with the option to upgrade to Canva for Work for $12.95 per month or $9.95 per month if you pay for the entire year.

- **PicMonkey** (www.picmonkey.com) – an easy to use photo-editing platform that also gives the option to add text. There is a free 7-day trial for the paid plan, which is $7.99 per month or $47.88 per year for premium and $8.33 per month or $99.99 per year for supremium. However, you can use the free option by scrolling down and clicking on 'edit photo.'

CHAPTER 7

CONTENT DO'S AND DON'TS

TYPE OF POSTS

As a general guideline, here is a variety of post types to get your creative juices flowing. Keep in mind that posting content can be a trial and error experience. See what does well and know you have the latitude to switch up whenever you choose.

- Tips/Advice – share your expertise. Everyone is good at something.
- Inspiration – repost a quote from someone else (give credit where credit is due) or create a quote using your wisdom.
- Fun – post funny memes. There are lots to choose from on Google Images.

- Resources – share a website, article, or book that your audience will appreciate.
- Frequently Asked Questions – think about the questions you often answer and turn those into a post.
- Testimonials – post testimonials from your customers/clients. Viewers like to know that other people have had good experiences with you.
- Industry News – post updates about new happenings your audience would appreciate.
- Spark conversation – post a controversial question related to your industry.
- Business highlights – attending events, meetings, projects (i.e. making care packages for students, stuffing swag bags for events, etc.).
- How to do…something (instructional) – bake a cake, decorate a room, choose the right eyewear for the shape of your face, etc.
- Promotional – clearly promote your product or service.

WRITING YOUR CONTENT

Know the tone of your audience. For example, with youth, be a little more casual.

Be sure your tone fits your tagline or mission. For example, if your appeal as a church is to come as you are, the tone of your posts should be a little more practical and straightforward versus scripture heavy.

Check your grammar and correct typos. It is very easy to miss something, especially when you're typing on your phone. Read it at least once before posting. If grammar is not your strong suit, send it to someone who is good at it and ask for it to be proofed.

Use industry keywords in your bio and content. The majority of information you post on your accounts is searchable, with the exception of private posts (posts just for friends or friends of friends on Facebook) or posts on private accounts. Be natural in your writing but include search terms people will use to find someone offering your product or service.

Make time. Set aside at least two hours per week to create content. Schedule it into your calendar like you would any other meeting. If you can do it for others, you can do it for yourself. You are worth it!

CHAPTER 8

YOU'RE READY!

Your online presence is essential to the success and longevity of your business. It takes time to build a pipeline of potential customers/clients and additional time to convert them. Don't wait until you are in dire need of business to build this pipeline. Get started now.

However, take it a step further. Give your followers an opportunity to sign up for your email list so that you're not relying on social media to communicate. The biggest value is in your list of contacts. Also, remember to take your online relationships offline whenever possible. Social media is a great way to meet people and stay in touch, but it doesn't replace other forms of communication and relationship building.

Note: Social media changes constantly so over time the number of users on each platform, the location of features, types of features, and how to take particular actions may change.

You've got this! I know you will do well.

(In the remainder of this book, see worksheets for every social media platform discussed)

WORKSHEETS

FACEBOOK PUBLIC PAGE WORKSHEET

The name of my public page is:

_____

My page category is:

_____

My Ideal Bio aka 'About' field is (155 characters):

— —

— —

— —

— —

— —

— —

— — — — — — — — —

Choose a dedicated day and time to write your content (schedule yourself into your calendar):

_____, _____
Day   Date

I commit to posting _____ times per day.

LINKEDIN WORKSHEET

My professional headline is (120 characters):

_____

_____

_____

_____

_____

_____

My Ideal Summary is:

(Reminder in 2,000 characters, tell a short story about who you are and what you offer)

_____

_____

_____

_____

_____

_____

_____

_____

_____

_____

_____

_____
_____
_____
_____
_____
_____
_____
_____
_____
_____
_____
_____
_____

My custom URL is
(www.linkedin.com/in/insertyourcustomURLhere):
(5 - 30 characters, letters or numbers; no spaces, symbols or special characters)

_ _
_ _ _ _ _ _ _ _ _ _

Choose a dedicated day and time to write your content
(schedule yourself into your calendar):

_____, _____

Day   Date

I commit to posting _____ times per day.

TWITTER WORKSHEET

My name is:

(20 character limit)

_____

My username is:

(15-character limit, no spaces, underscore permitted)

_____

My Ideal Bio is:

(160 character limit)

_____

_____

_____

_____

_____

_____

_____

_____

Choose a dedicated day and time to write your content (schedule yourself into your calendar):

_____, _____
      Day   Date

I commit to posting _____ times per day.

INSTAGRAM WORKSHEET

My name is:
(20 character limit)

_____

My username is:
(30 character limit; letters, numbers, periods, underscores only)

_____

_____

My Ideal Bio is:
(150 character limit)

_____

_____

_____

_____

_____

_____

_____

_____

Choose a dedicated day and time to write your content (schedule yourself into your calendar):

_____, _____
Day   Date

I commit to posting _____ times per day.

PERISCOPE WORKSHEET

When logging in using your Twitter account, Periscope auto-populates your Twitter info. You have the option to edit it or leave it the same.

My name is:
(20 character limit)

_____

My username is:
(15-character limit, no spaces, underscore permitted. If you log in with a phone number, your username must be a minimum of two characters.)

_____

My Ideal Bio is:
(160 character limit)

_____

_____

_____

_____

_____

_____

_____

Choose a dedicated day and time to write your topics with several talking points for each (schedule yourself into your calendar):

_____, _____
Day   Date

Check the Periscope scheduling format you will use:

☐ One set day and time per week plus two spontaneous Periscopes.

☐ One set time three times per week.

☐ All periscopes are spontaneous.

I commit to periscoping _____ times per week.

PINTEREST WORKSHEET

My account name is:
(38 character limit)

_____

_____

My username is:
(15 character limit)

_____

My Ideal Bio is:
(160 character limit)

_____

_____

_____

_____

_____

_____

_____

_____

Choose a dedicated day and time to write your content (schedule yourself into your calendar):

_____, _____
Day   Date

I commit to posting _____ **times per week.**

SNAPCHAT WORKSHEET

My username is:
(30 character limit)

__ __

__ __ __ __ __ __ __ __ __

Choose a dedicated day and time to look at your calendar for snapchat opportunities in addition to those spontaneous snaps and to write short statements for video snaps (schedule yourself into your calendar):

_____, _____

Day   Date

I commit to snapping _____ times per week.

GOOGLE+ WORKSHEET

Keep in mind that your Google+ account is connected to a Gmail address, so you will have to create or use an existing Gmail account. When you create a personal Google+ account, it will pull the name associated with that Gmail address. When you create a business Google+ account, you will be able to enter your business name regardless of the Gmail account you use.

My tagline is:
(140 character limit)

___ ___ ___ ___ ___ ___ ___ ___ ___ ___ ___ ___ ___ ___ ___

___ ___ ___ ___ ___ ___ ___ ___ ___ ___ ___ ___ ___ ___ ___

___ ___ ___ ___ ___ ___ ___ ___ ___ ___ ___ ___ ___ ___ ___

___ ___ ___ ___ ___ ___ ___ ___ ___ ___ ___ ___ ___ ___ ___

___ ___ ___ ___ ___ ___ ___ ___ ___ ___ ___ ___ ___ ___ ___

___ ___ ___ ___ ___ ___ ___ ___ ___ ___ ___ ___ ___ ___ ___

___ ___ ___ ___ ___ ___ ___ ___ ___ ___ ___

My Ideal Company Overview is:
(The space allotted for this is extensive, so have fun, but be sure to get to the point)

_____

_____

_____

_____

_____

_____

_____

_____

_____

_____

_____

_____

_____

_____

_____

_____

_____

_____

_____

_____

_____

_____

Choose a dedicated day and time to write your content (schedule yourself into your calendar):

_____, _____
Day   Date

I commit to posting _____ times per week.

YELP WORKSHEET
Checklist:

- _____ Menus added
- _____ Photos, videos added
- _____ Check-in offers added
- _____ Contact information (i.e. address, phone, website, etc.) added
- _____ All applicable business fields completed (i.e. parking, wifi, etc.)
- _____ Reservations set up (if applicable)
- _____ I commit to having staff ask each customer/client to leave us a review

I commit to checking Yelp _____ times per week.

I commit to adding updated information _____ times per week.

Let's Connect on Social Media

Facebook: Suzzette Turnbull (/SuzTurnbull)
Instagram: @suzyturn
Twitter: @suzyturn
Periscope: @suzyturn
Snapchat: @suzyturn
LinkedIn: Suzzette Turnbull
Website: www.suzytalks.com

Made in the USA
Middletown, DE
12 May 2018